Sally

Lehrwerk für den
Englischunterricht ab Klasse 1

Pupil's Book 4

Erarbeitet von
Martina Bredenbröcker
Jasmin Brune
Daniela Elsner
Barbara Gleich
Stefanie Gleixner-Weyrauch
Simone Gutwerk
Marion Lugauer
Sabine Schwarz

Unter Beratung von Jane Brockmann-Fairchild

Illustriert von
Monica May, Wilfried Poll,
Anja Boretzki, Andreas Fischer,
Thilo Pustlauk und Gisela Vogel

Oldenbourg

Inhalt

Special days:

pupil's CD / teacher's CD

teacher's CD only

Write.

Draw.

Speak.

Rap: Welcome back to school!

Susan

Tim

Step to the left, step to the right.

Raise your  and feel alright.

Turn around and say: "That's cool!"

Welcome back to school!

Eric

Emily

Sit on your , write in the air.

Let's have fun with English.

Dance to the beat and say: "That's cool!"

Welcome back to school!

Around the classroom you must look.

Put your  on the .

Turn around and say: "That's cool!"

Welcome back to school!

Phil

Liz

Let's rap!

 Listen and sing.

Let's play a board game!

Play in groups (2−5).
Roll the dice. Take turns.

Red number:
Do what it says or answer the question.
If you can't, miss a turn.

The winner is the first to reach finish.

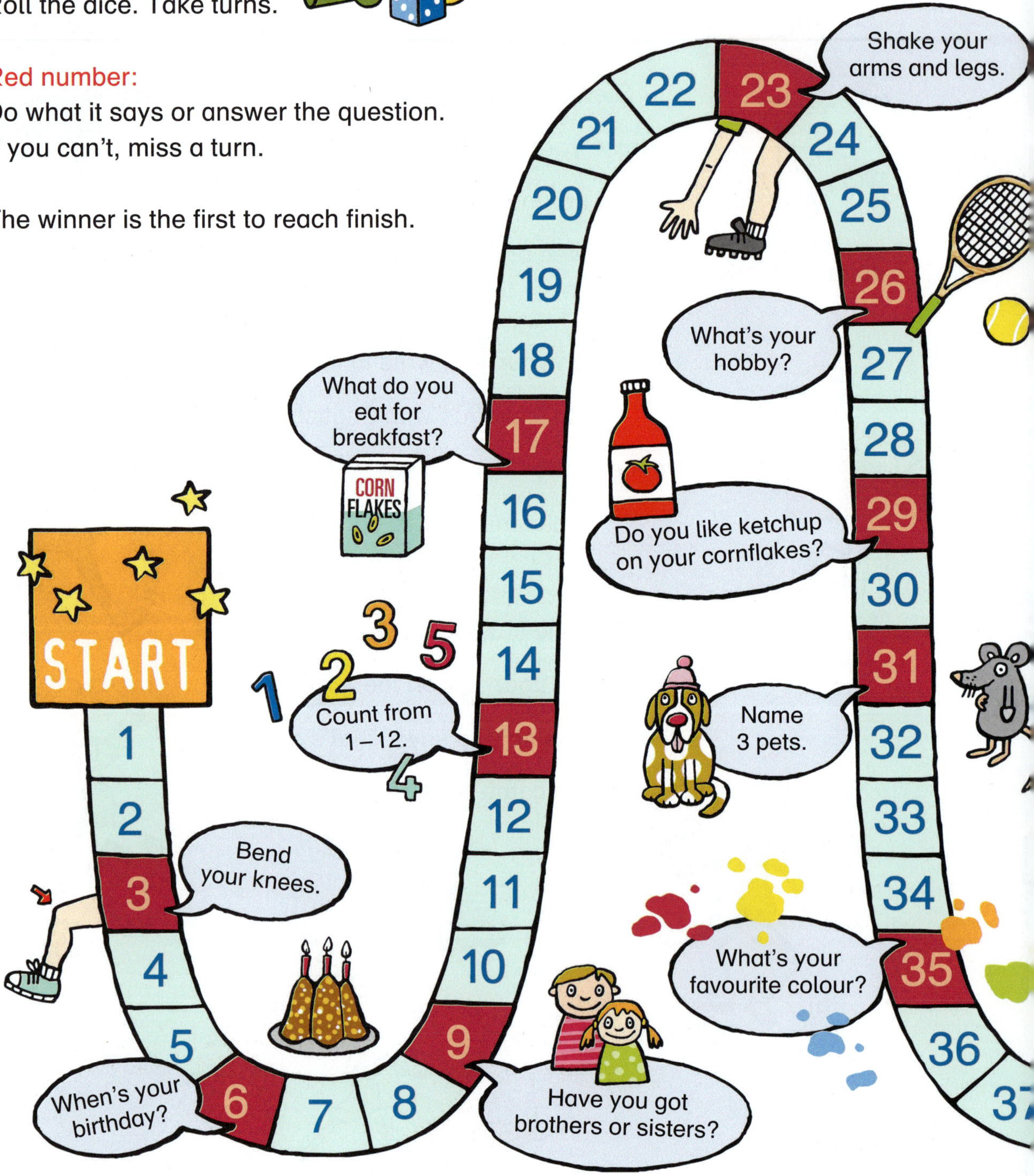

START

1
2
3 — Bend your knees.
4
5
When's your birthday?
6
7
8
9 — Have you got brothers or sisters?
10
11
12
13 — Count from 1−12.
14
15
16
17 — What do you eat for breakfast?

CORN FLAKES

18
19
20
21
22
23 — Shake your arms and legs.
24
25
26 — What's your hobby?
27
28
29 — Do you like ketchup on your cornflakes?
30
31 — Name 3 pets.
32
33
34
35 — What's your favourite colour?
36
37

At home

Our home is too small

bedroom   bedroom   bathroom

garden

kitchen   living room   toilet

The ... is too small!

My dream house has got a big garden, seven bedrooms ...

1. Listen to the story and point.

2. Look at the house and speak.
   The living room is too small …

3. Draw your dream house.
   Write about it.

Tim and Susan's new house

bed, chair, table,
desk, sofa,
cupboard, shelves,
stereo, lamp

door

window

My home is
my castle.

1. Listen, find Susan's furniture and point.

2. What furniture has Susan got?
   Susan has got brown shelves, a purple sofa …

3. What furniture have you got in your room?
   I've got …

Let's make Sally's sandwich!

You need:
bread
ketchup
mustard
a tomato
a cucumber
ham
cheese
lettuce

Take a slice of bread.
Put it on a plate.

Spread ketchup and
mustard on it.

Cut the tomato and
the cucumber.
Put them on the bread.

Put some ham, cheese
and lettuce on it.

Put another slice of
bread on top.

Cut the sandwich in
half. Sally's sandwich
is ready to eat!

What do you want to put on your sandwich?
Make a list.

Enjoy
your meal!

Let's have lunch

In the dining hall

It's Monday.

It's Tuesday.

It's Thursday.

It's Friday.

 1. Listen and read.

 2. Write about Phil's menu plan.
On Monday Phil has salad with cheese and a glass of water.
On Tuesday he has …

Emily's day

At 8 o'clock I get up
and have breakfast.

School begins
at 9 o'clock.

At 12 o'clock
I have lunch.

At 3 o'clock
I go home.

At 4 o'clock
I do my homework.

At 5 o'clock I call my
friends and we play
football.

At 6 o'clock
I have dinner.

At 8 o'clock I read
a book or watch TV.

At 9 o'clock I go to bed.
Good night!

1. Listen, look and read.

2. What about your day? Tell your partner what you do.
   In the morning …
   In the afternoon …
   In the evening / At night …

3. And what do you do on a Sunday?

> MY SUNDAY
> On Sunday I get up …

Hobbies

riding a horse   riding a mountain bike   playing the guitar
reading books   ice skating   playing the piano   snowboarding
playing football   swimming

1. What are their hobbies? Look and speak.
   Tim's hobby is …

2. What's your hobby?
   My hobby is …

3. Hobbies in your class:
   Make a list and do
   a class survey.

Teddy bear, teddy bear, turn around!

skipping

playing football ⚽ ⷭ l

reading books 📖 ⷭ

The interview

1. Ask your partner.

Yes, I can.

Can you ...?

No, I can't.

	play football	
	sing a song	
Can you	play the guitar	?
	ride a skateboard	
	do inline skating	

2. Listen to the interview with Dirk Nowitzki.

Dirk Nowitzki is playing basketball.

 3. Do your own interview.

 4. Say the tongue twister.

I can canoe a new canoe.
Can you canoe a new canoe, too?

In the supermarket

SPECIAL OFFER

CHOCOLATE BARS

BREAD   ROLLS

BISCUITS   JAM

COFFEE   TEA

DRINKS

LEMONADES

JUICE

PAY HERE!

SUPER MARKET

SUPER MARKET

MILK

CHEESE

BUTTER   EGGS

HONEY

PINEAPPLES

APPLES

BANANAS

LEMONS

CHERRIES

ORANGES

SPINACH

PEARS

1. Listen and point.

2. Make your own shopping list.
   I want to buy two bottles of orange juice,
   a box of biscuits …

Next time I'll take a cart.

Shopping

At the shopping centre

MUSIC SHOP

computer games

new CD by the Supergirls

SHOE SHOP

sale 59.- 29.-

BOOK SHOP

TOY SHOP

PC GAME

scrabble

PUZZLE

BESTSELLER

SUPERMARKET

RESTAURANT

HAM-BURGER

tea & coffee

coffee to go

SWEET SHOP | CINEMA

SPORTS SHOP | JEANS & SKIRTS

T-SHIRTS
£ 5
buy one – get one free

CAPS

COMPUTER SHOP

💬 1. Where can you buy these things?

book shop
sports shop
music shop
In the   supermarket   I can buy
toy shop
sweet shop
shoe shop

 2. Design your own shopping centre.

Jack and the beanstalk

1. Listen, look and point.

2. Act out the story together.

Let's act it out!

Reading and learning the story

Painting the background

Making the music

Telling the story with shadow puppets

Practising the story

Performing the story

The Wright Brothers

The Wright Brothers made bikes.

The Wright Brothers made kites.

The Wright Brothers made planes.

The Wright Brothers became famous with the "Wright Model B".

1. Look and read.

a bike saucer

a flying sledge

a one-wheeled car

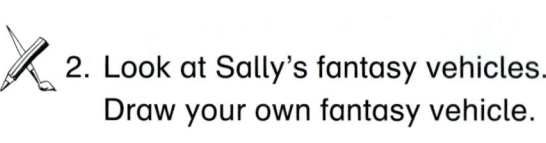

I want to fly like the Wright Brothers!

2. Look at Sally's fantasy vehicles. Draw your own fantasy vehicle.

In the plane

 No smoking!

 Switch off your mobile phones, radios and laptops!

 Fasten your seat belts, please!

 Put your seats in an upright position!

 1. Listen and point.

 2. Draw your own sign. Ask your partner: What is it?

Transport in London

left-hand traffic with
double-decker buses

a taxi

an entrance to the underground trains

a ferry on the River Thames

 3. Look at the photos. What's different in England?

Detective Brighthead

It's a thief!

Let's follow him!

To the River Thames, please!

Tibby, let's take the ferry, too!

A ticket to Queens Road, please!

Let's catch him!

1. Listen to the story and look at the pictures.

2. What forms of transport does Mr Brighthead take? He takes the ...

Detective Brighthead's trip to the jungle

zebra   lion   giraffe   hippo

monkey   elephant   snake   tortoise

1. **Where are the animals?**
   Ask your partner.

   Is the zebra next to the snake?
   Is the hippo behind the elephant? ...

   | in   on   next to   in front of |
   | behind   under |

   (Yes, it is.)   (No, it isn't. It's ...)

 2. **Make a poster.**

The clever tortoise

Listen, look and read.

The five minute zoo game

Play with a partner.

Roll the dice.

Play for five minutes.

Take turns.

The winner is the player who has got the most points.

START

Move in any direction.

Animal picture:
Name the animal = 1 point.
Name the animal and describe it = 2 points.

Snack stop: You must pay. Miss a turn.

Crocodile: Bad luck! You lose 1 point.

At the doctor's

I'm sick. My ear hurts. I've got an earache.

DOCTOR
C. ROC

Next,
please!

I'm fine, thanks.

I'm sick. My neck hurts. I've got a neckache.

DOCTOR
C. ROC

Next,
please!

I'm fine, thank you.

1. Read.

2. Why do the animals run away each time? Look at the green door.

The inline skating accident

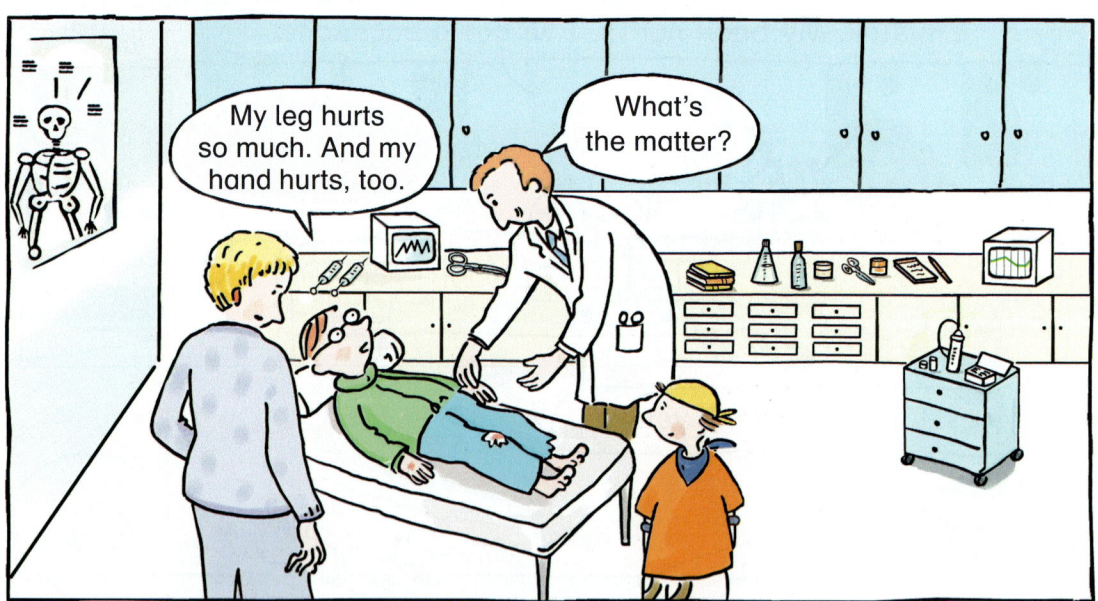

1. Look and speak.

2. Look at the waiting room.
   What's the matter?
   Write a sentence about each patient.
   The boy has got a headache ...

| headache |
| neckache |
| earache |
| backache |

An apple a day keeps the doctor away.

Going to Scotland

Sally and the Loch Ness Monster

A photo of Loch Ness Monster!

Welcome!

Hello!

Where is Nessie?

Where is Nessie?

Goodbye, uncle!

Robert, Sally, look at this photo!

There's Nessie in the lake!

Listen, look and read.

A holiday trip to Scotland

I want to see the Highland Mountains and go fishing.

I want to go to a castle.

I want to visit the Highland Games.

I want to go to the sea.

And we all want to see Nessie!

1. Look and speak. Mr Brown wants to see …

2. Make a poster or a collage about Scotland.
   Find out and learn about Scotland on the internet.

3. Where do you want to go for your holidays?

Going to Scotland

Scottish dance

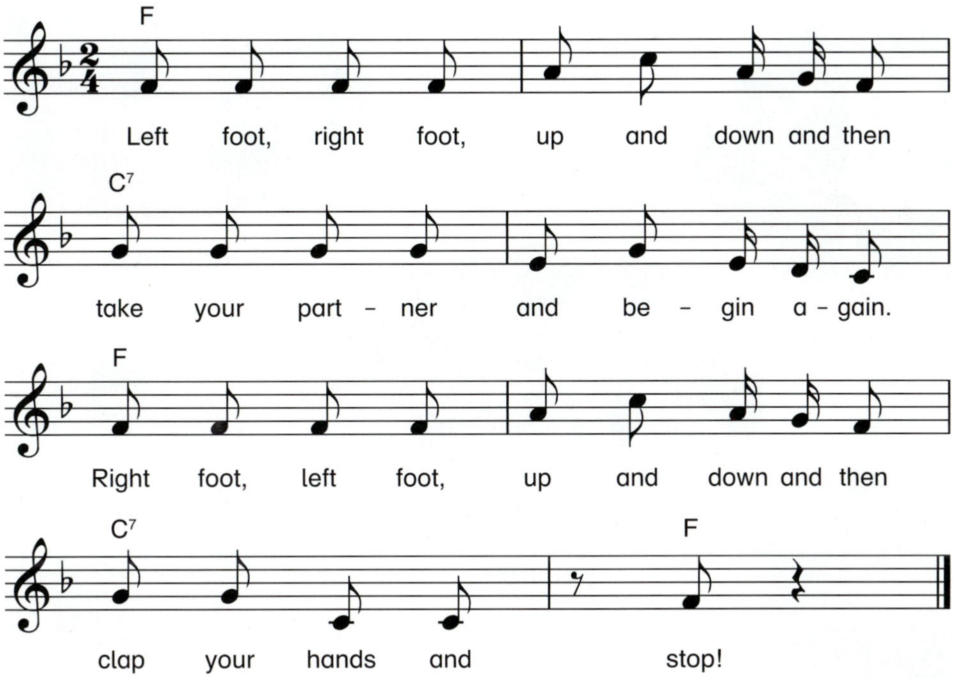

Left foot, right foot, up and down and then take your part – ner and be – gin a – gain.

Right foot, left foot, up and down and then clap your hands and stop!

Today I'm wearing my kilt.

Listen, sing and dance.

What do you want to be?

shop assistant

hairdresser

policewoman

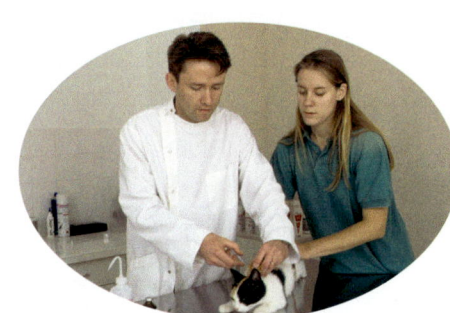

teacher

vet

doctor

football player

 1. Listen and point.

 2. What do you want to be?
   I want to be a ...

 3. Do a job survey in your class.
   Make a chart.

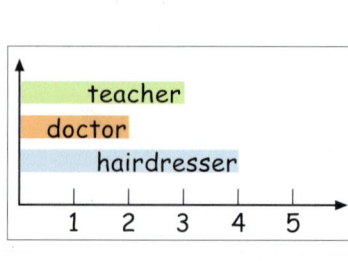

I want to be a superstar!

My jobs

I have to help in the garden.

I have to make my bed.

I have to do my homework.

I have to feed the cat.

I have to walk the dog.

I have to tidy my room.

I have to help in the kitchen.

And what are your jobs?
I have to …

My cat likes to hide in boxes

Japan

France

Spain

Berlin, Germany

Greece

 1. Listen and look.

 2. Mime one of the cats.
Let your partner guess.

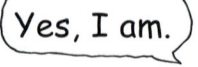 Are you from ...?

 Yes, I am.

No, I'm not.

We all live in the same world

Hola!

Juanita

Bonjour!

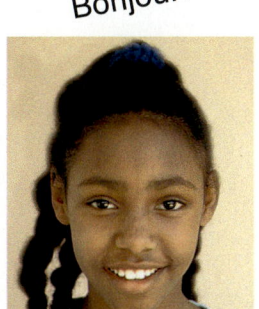

Jacqueline

Ciao!

Paolo

Hello!

Thomas

Hallo!

Maria

Merhaba!

Güler

Jassu!

Dimitra

Priwjet!

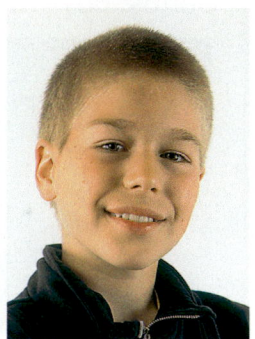

Sergej

But we all laugh in the same language.
We all like to sing and play.
We all live in the same world,
no matter where we're from.

 1. Listen and sing.

2. What's the word for ⟨ Hello! ⟩
   in different languages?
   Make a list.

Are you from Japan, too?

No, I'm not. I'm from Australia!

Looking for a penfriend

Find a penfriend!

I'm a boy .   I'm 8 years old.   I'm from Germany .
        girl   9   England
                        10   Australia

My hobby is snowboarding .

I'm looking for a boy .   Age: 8   Country: USA
                   girl   9   Germany
                                 10   Spain

Carlos: boy, 10 years old, Spain

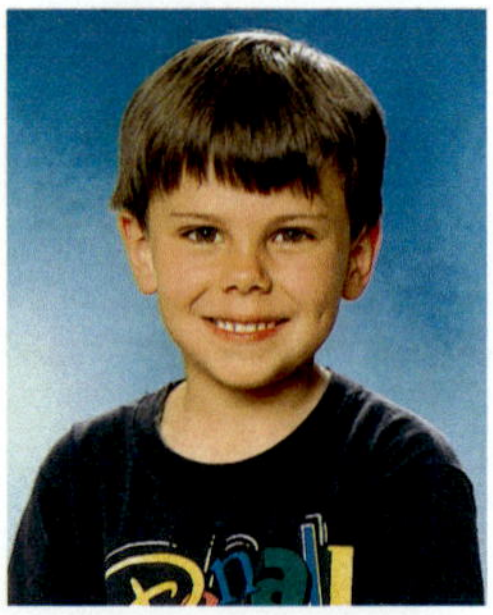

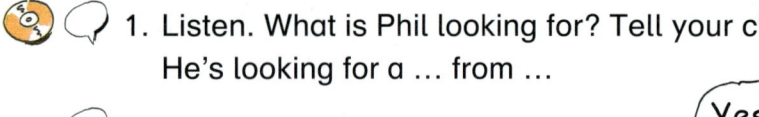

Hi, I'm Carlos. I'm from Spain.
I'm 10 years old.
My hobbies are skateboarding,
reading comics and swimming.
I can speak Spanish, German and English.
I'm looking for a penfriend from England.

1. Listen. What is Phil looking for? Tell your class.
   He's looking for a … from …

2. Are you looking for a penfriend, too?   *Yes, I'm looking for a …*   *No, I don't want a penfriend.*
   Tell your partner.

3. Write a letter to Carlos.

   Dear Carlos,
   I'm …

   Where is the mouse? I want to catch it.

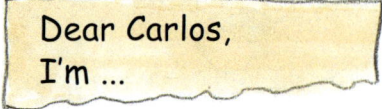

 **Guy Fawkes**

Guy Fawkes Day – Bonfire Night

Light the fire, light the fire.
Let it burn, let it burn.
Bonfire, bonfire.
Guy Fawkes Day, Guy Fawkes Day.

Sizzle, whistle, sizzle, whistle.
Crackle, rumble, crackle, rumble.
Boom, bang, boom, bang.
Fireworks, fireworks.

1. Listen and sing.

2. Write the seasons in the correct order.
   spring, …

  winter  summer

 autumn   spring

Thanksgiving today

Mum gets up at 6 o'clock
in the morning.
She puts the turkey into the oven.
The turkey takes five hours to cook.

At 12 o'clock my grandpa,
my grandma, my aunt and
my cousins come to our house.
We have our Thanksgiving dinner.

In the afternoon we go to the
Thanksgiving parade.

In the evening we watch the football
match on TV.

> My name is Carol.
> This is my
> Thanksgiving Day.
> What do you celebrate
> in your country?

> A turkey is a funny bird,
> his head goes wobble, wobble.
> And he knows just one word:
> "Gobble, gobble, gobble!"

 Listen, look and read.

A story about the first Thanksgiving

The first Thanksgiving

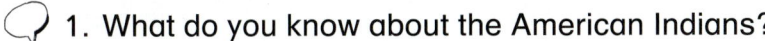

1. What do you know about the American Indians?

2. What is Sally writing?

Come to the USA!

New York and the Statue of Liberty

Disney World, Florida (fun park)

a cowboy at work

Bryce Canyon National Park, Utah

a cable car in San Francisco

Venice Beach, Los Angeles

1. Look at the photos.

 2. Make a poster or a collage about the USA.
    Find out and learn about the USA on the internet.

Father Christmas in Australia

It's too hot! The reindeer can't pull the sleigh.

Can we help you?

Stop! Stop!

I've got a good idea!

Merry Christmas!

 1. Listen and point.

2. Read.

The five days of Christmas

On the first day of Christmas
my true love sent to me
a  in a gum tree.

On the second day of Christmas
my true love sent to me

two small [koala images]

and a [kookaburra image] in a gum tree.

kookaburra

koala

On the third day of Christmas
my true love sent to me

three [cockatoo images] ,

two small …

cockatoo

On the fourth day of Christmas
my true love sent to me

four [crocodile images] ,

three …

crocodile

On the fifth day of Christmas
my true love sent to me

five [kangaroo images] ,

four …

kangaroo

1. Look at the photos. Listen and sing.

2. Write word cards for a Christmas bingo.
   sleigh, reindeer, stocking, present, star,
   Christmas tree, winter, cold, snowy...

Let's go to Australia!

Sydney is the biggest city.

A road train is a very long truck.

Ayers Rock is a big flat rock.

At the Great Barrier Reef
you can see under water corals
and wonderful coloured fish.

An Australian Aborigine
is playing the didgeridoo.

1. Look at the photos.

 2. Listen and point.

3. Read the text. Find the correct photo.

4. Draw an Australian traffic sign.

G'day!

Let's make an Easter bunny mosaic card!

You need:
coloured eggshells
cardboard
a pencil
glue
scissors

Break the eggshells
into small pieces.

Draw your Easter bunny
on the cardboard. Cut it out.

Glue the eggshells down
to make your mosaic bunny.

Glue your Easter bunny onto the
cardboard. Write an Easter greeting
on your card.

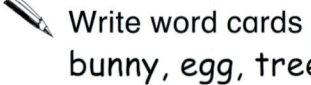 Write word cards for an Easter bingo.
bunny, egg, tree, flower, grass,
spring, warm, cloudy, sunny, ...

Words

Africa   Afrika
afternoon   der Nachmittag
America   Amerika
I am   ich bin
angry   wütend
animal   das Tier
animal centre   das Tierheim
apple   der Apfel
April   der April
they are   sie sind
we are   wir sind
you are   du bist, ihr seid
arm   der Arm
arrow   der Pfeil
Asia   Asien
August   der August
aunt   die Tante
Australia   Australien
autumn   der Herbst
away   weg

backache   die Rückenschmerzen
bacon   der Speck
bad   schlecht, schlimm
ball   der Ball
banana   die Banane
basket   der Korb
bat   die Fledermaus
bathroom   das Badezimmer
to be   sein
beach   der Strand
beach ball   der Wasserball
bean   die Bohne
beanstalk   die Bohnenranke

bear   der Bär
bed   das Bett
bedroom   das Schlafzimmer
behind   hinter
to bend   beugen
big   groß
bird   der Vogel
birthday   der Geburtstag
biscuit   der Keks
black   schwarz
blood   das Blut
blue   blau
board   die Tafel
body   der Körper
book   das Buch
boot   der Stiefel
bottle   die Flasche
bow   der Bogen
box (boxes)   die Schachtel
(die Schachteln), die Kiste (die Kisten)
boy   der Junge
bread   das Brot
breakfast   das Frühstück
brother   der Bruder
brown   braun
to brush   bürsten
budgie   der Wellensittich
bus (buses)   der Bus (die Busse)
butter   die Butter
to buy   kaufen

cake   der Kuchen
to call   rufen, anrufen
can   können
can't   nicht können
Canada   Kanada
candle   die Kerze
cap   die Kappe

Words

car das Auto

card die Karte

carrot die Karotte, die Möhre

castle das Schloss, die Burg

cat die Katze

to catch fangen

chair der Stuhl

chalk die Kreide

cheap billig

cheese der Käse

cherry (cherries)

die Kirsche (die Kirschen)

child das Kind

children die Kinder

chimney der Schornstein

chocolate bar der Schokoriegel

Christmas Weihnachten

Christmas tree

der Weihnachtsbaum, der Christbaum

to clap klatschen

class die Klasse

to clean putzen

clever schlau, klug

to climb klettern, hochklettern

(one) o'clock (ein) Uhr

clothes die Kleidung

cloud die Wolke

cloudy bewölkt

coat der Mantel

coffee der Kaffee

coke die Cola

cold kalt

colour die Farbe

to colour anmalen

to come kommen

computer der Computer

computer game das Computerspiel

cookie der Keks

corn der Mais

cornflakes die Cornflakes

costume die Verkleidung

to count zählen

cousin der Cousin, die Cousine

cow die Kuh

cucumber die Gurke

a cup of ... eine Tasse ...

cupboard der Schrank

to cut schneiden

to dance tanzen

dark dunkel

day der Tag

December der Dezember

desk der Schreibtisch

dice der Würfel

dirty schmutzig

to do machen, tun

to do magic zaubern

doctor der Arzt

dog der Hund

doll die Puppe

door die Tür

down hinunter

to draw zeichnen

dress das Kleid

drink das Getränk

to drink trinken

duck die Ente

ear das Ohr

earache die Ohrenschmerzen

Easter Ostern

Easter bunny der Osterhase

Easter egg das Osterei

to eat essen

egg das Ei

eight acht

Words

elephant   der Elefant

eleven   elf

England   England

English   englisch

Englishman   der Engländer

Europe   Europa

evening   der Abend

exercise   die Übung

expensive   teuer

eye   das Auge

fairy   die Fee

family   die Familie

farm animal   das Bauernhoftier

fast   schnell

fat   dick, fett

father   der Vater

Father Christmas
der Weihnachtsmann

favourite (pet)   Lieblings(tier)

February   der Februar

to feed   füttern

feet   die Füße

ferry   die Fähre

to fill   füllen

fine   gut, schön

finger   der Finger

fireplace   der Kamin

fish   der Fisch, die Fische

five   fünf

floor   der Fußboden

flower   die Blume

fly   die Fliege

to fly   fliegen

fog   der Nebel

foggy   nebelig

folder   der Schnellhefter

food   das Essen

foot   der Fuß

football   der Fußball

forest   der Wald

fork   die Gabel

four   vier

France   Frankreich

Friday   der Freitag

friend   der Freund, die Freundin

friendly   freundlich

frog   der Frosch

fruit   die Frucht, das Obst

fruit salad   der Obstsalat

fun   der Spaß

funny   lustig, komisch

game   das Spiel

garage   die Garage

garden   der Garten

German   deutsch

Germany   Deutschland

to get up   aufstehen

ghost   der Geist

giraffe   die Giraffe

girl   das Mädchen

a glass of ...   ein Glas ...

glue   der Kleber

to go   gehen, fahren

good   gut

goose   die Gans

grandfather   der Großvater

grandmother   die Großmutter

grass   das Gras

Great Britain   Großbritannien

green   grün

grey   grau

guard   die Wache

guinea pig   das Meerschweinchen

guitar   die Gitarre

Words

hair das Haar
Halloween Halloween
ham der Schinken
hamster der Hamster
hand die Hand
happy glücklich
hat der Hut
to have (got) haben
to have (lunch) (zu Mittag) essen
head der Kopf
headache die Kopfschmerzen
to help helfen
hen die Henne
hill der Hügel
hippo das Nilpferd
holidays die Ferien
hobby (hobbies) das Hobby
(die Hobbys)
home das Heim, das Zuhause
at home zu Hause
homework die Hausaufgaben
honey der Honig
horse das Pferd
hot chocolate der Kakao
hot heiß
house das Haus
hungry hungrig
to hurt wehtun

ice cream das Eis
ice skating das Schlittschuhfahren
in front of vor
in in
inline skates die Inlineskates
insect das Insekt

jacket die Jacke
jam die Marmelade
January der Januar
Japan Japan
jeans die Jeans
job die Arbeit, die Aufgabe
July der Juli
to jump springen
June der Juni

kangaroo das Känguru
ketchup das Ketchup
king der König
kitchen die Küche
knee das Knie
knife (knives) das Messer (die Messer)
to knock klopfen
to know wissen, kennen

Words

ladder   die Leiter
lake   der See
lamp   die Lampe
leaf (leaves)   das Blatt (die Blätter)
to learn   lernen
left   links
leg   das Bein
lemon   die Zitrone
lemonade   die Limonade
letter   der Brief
lettuce   der Kopfsalat
to like   mögen
lion   der Löwe
to listen (to)   zuhören
little   klein
to live   leben, wohnen
living room   das Wohnzimmer
to love   lieben, sehr mögen
lunch   das Mittagessen

magic (beans)   Zauber(bohnen)
to make   machen
March   der März
market   der Markt
May   der Mai
meadow   die Wiese
to meet   treffen, begegnen
melon   die Melone
mice   die Mäuse
milk   die Milch
mitten   der Fäustling
Monday   der Montag
money   das Geld
monkey   der Affe
month   der Monat

monster   das Ungeheuer
moon   der Mond
morning   der Morgen
mother   die Mutter
mountain   der Berg
mountain bike   das Mountainbike
mouse   die Maus
mouth   der Mund
to move   (sich) bewegen
must   müssen
mustard   der Senf

name   der Name
neckache   die Nackenschmerzen
new   neu
New Zealand   Neuseeland
next to   neben
night   die Nacht
nine   neun
nose   die Nase
November   der November
number   die Zahl

October   der Oktober
old   alt
on   auf
one   eins
orange   die Orange; orange
orange juice   der Orangensaft

Words

to paint malen
palace der Palast
parents die Eltern
park der Park
to pay bezahlen
pear die Birne
pen der Füller
pencil der Bleistift
pencil case das Mäppchen
people die Leute, die Menschen
pepper der Pfeffer
pet das Haustier
piano das Klavier
picture das Bild
pie die Pastete, der Kuchen
pig das Schwein
pineapple die Ananas
pink rosa
plane das Flugzeug
plate der Teller
to play spielen
player der Spieler
please bitte
plum die Pflaume
pond der Teich
poor arm
potato (potatoes)
die Kartoffel (die Kartoffeln)
present das Geschenk
prince der Prinz
princess die Prinzessin
pullover der Pullover
pumpkin der Kürbis
pupil der Schüler
purple lila
to put setzen, stellen, legen
to put on anziehen

queen die Königin

rabbit das Kaninchen
rain der Regen
rainy regnerisch
to read lesen
red rot
reindeer das Rentier, die Rentiere
rich reich
to ride fahren, reiten
right rechts
river der Fluss
roll das Brötchen, die Semmel
room das Zimmer
rubber der Radiergummi
ruler das Lineal
to run rennen, laufen

sad traurig
salt das Salz
sand der Sand
sandwich das Sandwich
Saturday der Samstag
scared erschrocken, ängstlich
scarf der Schal
school die Schule
schoolbag die Schultasche
scissors die Schere
Scotland Schottland
sea das Meer, die See
seashell die Muschel

Words

season   die Jahreszeit

to see   sehen

to sell   verkaufen

September   der September

seven   sieben

to shake   schütteln

sheep   das Schaf

shelves   das Regal

sheriff   der Sheriff

to shine   scheinen

ship   das Schiff

shoe   der Schuh

shop   das Geschäft, der Laden

shopping   der Einkauf, das Einkaufen

short   kurz

shorts   die kurze Hose

shoulder   die Schulter

to show   zeigen

sick   krank

to sing   singen

sister   die Schwester

six   sechs

skirt   der Rock

sleigh   der (Pferde-)Schlitten

slow   langsam

small   klein

to smell   riechen

snake   die Schlange

to snorkel   schnorcheln, tauchen

snow   der Schnee

snowboarding   das Snowboarden

snowman   der Schneemann

snowy   verschneit

sock   die Socke

sofa   das Sofa

song   das Lied

I'm sorry!   Entschuldigung!

soup   die Suppe

spaceship   das Raumschiff

Spain   Spanien

to speak   sprechen

spider   die Spinne

spinach   der Spinat

spoon   der Löffel

sports   Sport

spring   der Frühling

stairs   die Treppe

to stamp   stampfen

star   der Stern

stereo   die Musikanlage

stocking   der Strumpf

story   die Geschichte

strong   stark

sugar   der Zucker

summer   der Sommer

sun   die Sonne

Sunday   der Sonntag

sunglasses   die Sonnenbrille

sunny   sonnig

sweatshirt   das Sweatshirt

sweet   süß

sweets   die Süßigkeiten

to swim   schwimmen

table   der Tisch

tadpole   die Kaulquappe

to take   nehmen

to take off   ausziehen

tall   groß

taxi   das Taxi

tea   der Tee

teacher   der Lehrer, die Lehrerin

teddy bear   der Teddybär

teeth   die Zähne

ten   zehn

Thank you!   Danke!

Thanksgiving Day   das Erntedankfest

thirsty   durstig

three   drei

Words

Thursday der Donnerstag
to tidy aufräumen, saubermachen
tired müde
toast der Toast
toe der Zeh
toilet die Toilette, das Klo
tomato (tomatoes)
die Tomate (die Tomaten)
tooth der Zahn
tortoise die Schildkröte
to touch anfassen
towel das Handtuch
toy das Spielzeug
train der Zug
tree der Baum
trousers die Hose
T-shirt das T-Shirt
Tuesday der Dienstag
turkey der Truthahn
twelve zwölf
two zwei

uncle der Onkel
under unter
underground die U-Bahn
unhappy unglücklich
Union Jack britische Fahne
United States of America
die Vereinigten Staaten von Amerika,
die USA
up hinauf

Valentine's Day der Valentinstag
vehicle das Fahrzeug, das Verkehrsmittel

to walk gehen, wandern
to walk the dog
den Hund spazieren führen
to write schreiben
warm warm
water das Wasser
to wash waschen
wax figure die Wachsfigur
to wear tragen
weather das Wetter
weather forecast
die Wettervorhersage
Wednesday der Mittwoch
white weiß
wild wild
wind der Wind
window das Fenster
windy windig
winter der Winter
witch die Hexe
woolly hat die Mütze
word das Wort
workbook das Arbeitsheft

yellow gelb